BORIS

MIND THE GAP

Fun Guessing Game!

Colour in the London boroughs, representing crime statistics with your felt tips...

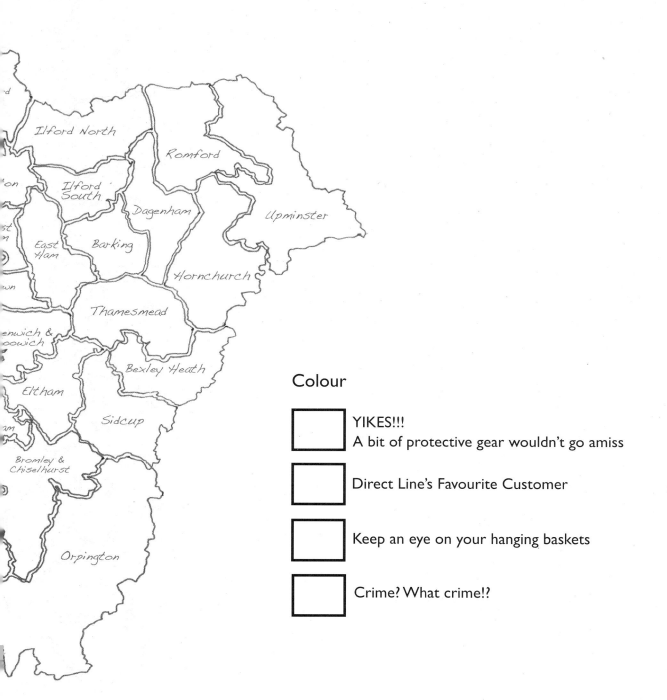

Ilford North

Romford

Ilford South

Dagenham

Upminster

East Ham

Barking

Hornchurch

Thamesmead

enwich &
oowich

Bexley Heath

Eltham

Sidcup

Bromley &
Chiselhurst

Orpington

Colour

YIKES!!!
A bit of protective gear wouldn't go amiss

Direct Line's Favourite Customer

Keep an eye on your hanging baskets

Crime? What crime!?

Colour Me Good - London
ISBN No:
978-0-9570056-2-4
Designed & Illustrated by
Mel Simone Elliott
© M S Elliott 2010
www.ilovemel.me